How to do verbal reasoning

Alison Primrose

Published in 2001 by:
Nelson Thornes Ltd
Delta Place
27 Bath Road
CHELTENHAM
GL53 7TH
United Kingdom

06 07 08 09 10 / 10 9 8 7

A catalogue record for this book is available from the British Library

ISBN 0-7487-6441-0

Page make-up by Green House Design

Printed and bound in Croatia by Zrinski

Introduction

About verbal reasoning

This book is a step-by-step guide to all the different types of questions commonly set in verbal reasoning tests up to 11+ and 12+ exams. It can be used on its own for practice and learning alongside any other verbal reasoning papers you might have. Or it may be used hand-in-hand with *Bond Assessment Papers in Reasoning*, which provide sets of graded papers for development and extensive practice of reasoning skills. All the questions in the Bond Papers are cross-referenced to this book so that you can use it as a tutorial for any questions that cause problems.

In general, verbal reasoning papers are set in two forms: standard format, where the answer is marked on the question paper, and multiple choice format, where you are given extra answer sheets and you tick a numbered choice to indicate your answer. This book, and the *Bond Assessment Papers*, follow the standard format. In general, the multiple choice format makes answering slightly easier as it gives you only a limited choice of answers to choose from. Getting used to multiple choice papers is easy once you are familiar with the verbal reasoning skills taught here.

Verbal reasoning questions are like word puzzles or games and they come in many different forms. This book identifies the 50 different types that are commonly set and explains the best way of tackling all of them. Verbal reasoning includes questions that test observation and reasoning at the letter, word and sentence level. They often require the answer to be selected from given options. Sometimes they require new words to be made or to be found. They require a good understanding of the meaning of words so that you can find similar words, or their opposites. Verbal reasoning tests often include some questions that involve mathematical calculations and which at first sight have nothing to do with words at all. They provide another way to develop reasoning skills and are covered in this book.

How to use this book

The book provides:
- coverage of the 50 most common types of verbal reasoning test question
- step-by-step strategies for tackling each type
- further questions of each type for more practice. You will find the answers to these at the back.

Each type works like this:

The title is a brief summary of what the type is about.

At the top of the page an example of the type is given.

This explains step-by-step how to tackle the example question. It begins with a short general statement explaining how to tackle questions of this kind.

This takes you step-by-step through the example question, explaining the best strategy for tackling it.

This gives you further questions to try in order to build up familiarity and confidence. You will find the answers in the back.

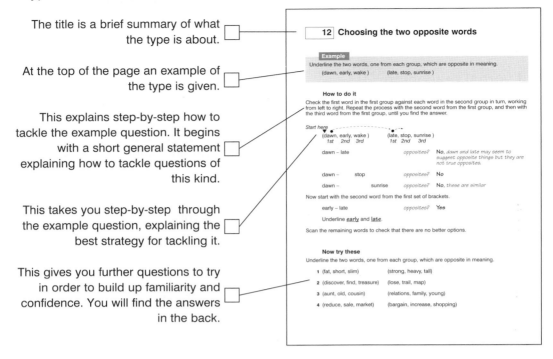

12 Choosing the two opposite words

Example

Underline the two words, one from each group, which are opposite in meaning.

(dawn, early, wake)   (late, stop, sunrise)

How to do it

Check the first word in the first group against each word in the second group in turn, working from left to right. Repeat the process with the second word from the first group, and then with the third word from the first group, until you find the answer.

Start here

(dawn, early, wake)   (late, stop, sunrise)
 1st   2nd   3rd   1st 2nd 3rd

dawn – late   opposites?   No, dawn and late may seem to suggest opposite things but they are not true opposites.

dawn – stop   opposites?   No

dawn – sunrise   opposites?   No, these are similar

Now start with the second word from the first set of brackets.

early – late   opposites?   Yes

Underline *early* and *late*.

Scan the remaining words to check that there are no better options.

Now try these

Underline the two words, one from each group, which are opposite in meaning.

1 (fat, short, slim)   (strong, heavy, tall)
2 (discover, find, treasure) (lose, trail, map)
3 (aunt, old, cousin)   (relations, family, young)
4 (reduce, sale, market)   (bargain, increase, shopping)

The keys to success in verbal reasoning

The key to success though with any type of reasoning question is through the development and application of two key skills – and two good habits!

Two key skills

1 *Read the question slowly and carefully*
Say each word 'aloud in your head' to ensure you do not misread any. If you find this hard, read them aloud to start with and change to silent reading when you are more confident with the question types.

2 *Work systematically from left to right*
It is very important to keep words or letters in the given order. To make sure that you have not missed or muddled any options always work from left to right, matching or checking each word across the page as you go.

Two good habits

1 *Use your pencil*
Don't be afraid of making notes or marks by the questions.
It is often helpful to cross out letters or words which you have eliminated as options. Put a single line through the letter or word so that it is still visible.
Drawing arrows or lines can help when trying to match letters or words, or when finding positions along the alphabet.

2 *Check your answers*
Unless you are very short of time, check your answer by re-reading the question and checking that your solution makes sense and does answer it.
When a number of options are given and the correct answer is found before reaching the final option, check the remaining options to check that there is no better answer available.

Identifying group features and sorting words into the groups

Look at these groups of words.

Group A	Group B	Group C	Group D
car	table	bread	stomach
bus	bookshelf	pancake	liver
lorry	stool	pizza	brain

Choose the correct group for each of the words below. Write the letter.

1 pasta C **2** bench B **3** sofa B **4** heart D **5** lungs __ **6** van __

Look carefully at each group, working from left to right.
Notice what each group has in common; you may think of more than one thing.
Then work through the listed words, in order, and match them to a group.
If you cannot do any of the words miss them out and come back to them later.

Start here
▼

Group A
car
bus   *transport   vehicles   four wheels*
lorry

Group B
table
bookshelf   *furniture   things found in the home*
stool

Group C
bread
pancake   *foods   from wheat / starchy foods*
pizza

Group D
stomach
liver   *parts of the body   internal organs*
brain

1 pasta? *food* <u>C</u>
2 bench? *to sit on, furniture* <u>B</u>
3 sofa? *furniture* <u>B</u>
4 heart? *internal organ* <u>D</u>
5 lungs? *part of the body* <u>D</u>
6 van? *transport* <u>A</u>

Now try these

1 Look at these groups of words.

Group A	Group B	Group C
red	coffee	hockey
orange	tea	football
blue	beer	tennis

Now choose the correct group for each of the words listed below. Write the letter.

basketball __   lemonade __   cricket __   green __   milk __   white __

2 Look at these groups of words.

Group A	Group B	Group C
flute	triangle	violin
recorder	xylophone	guitar
trumpet	tambour	cello

Now choose the correct group for each of the words listed below. Write the letter.

drum __   double bass __   clarinet __   oboe __   chime bar __   viola __

3 Look at these groups of words.

Group A	Group B	Group C
French	river	Poland
Spanish	stream	Austria
Latin	sea	Italy

Now choose the correct group for each of the words listed below. Write the letter.

German _A_   ocean _B_   Dutch _A_   Belgium _C_   lake _B_   Sweden _C_

4 Look at these groups of words.

Group A	Group B	Group C
jeans	soap	silk
coat	shower gel	nylon
cardigan	powder	leather

Now choose the correct group for each of the words listed below. Write the letter.

cotton __   shampoo __   shorts __   jumper __   velvet __   bath-oil __

2 | Sorting words into given groups

Write the following words in the correct groups.

dollar   pound   hammer   plate   saw   cent   teapot   cup   spanner

Money	Tools	Crockery → *kitchen china* .
dollar	hammer	plate
pound	saw	teapot
cent	spanner	cup

How to do it

Read the question carefully and then look at the three groups.
Look at each word in turn, read it and then place it in the correct group.
Work from left to right.

Start here
▼

dollar?   __money__

  pound?   __money__

    hammer?   __tools__

      plate?   __crockery__

       saw?   __tools__

        cent?   __money__

         teapot?   __crockery__

          cup?   __crockery__

           spanner?   __tools__

These questions rely on you knowing the words.
(If spaces are given, the number of spaces can give you a clue about how many words you need to put in each group.)

Now try these

Write the following words in the correct groups.

1 envelopes   roses   stamp   potato   daffodil   turnip   snowdrop   beetroot

Stationery	**Flowers**	**Vegetables**
_____	_____	_____
_____	_____	_____
	_____	_____

2 Chile   Thames   France   London   Paris   Severn

Rivers	**Countries**	**Cities**
_____	_____	_____
_____	_____	_____

3 dollars   minutes   francs   kilogrammes   hours   seconds   euros   grams   tonnes

Currency	**Measures of mass**	**Measures of time**
_____	_____	_____
_____	_____	_____
_____	_____	_____

4 wardrobe   bungalow   table   wood   mansion   plastic   steel   cottage   chair

Buildings	**Materials**	**Furniture**
_____	_____	_____
_____	_____	_____
_____	_____	_____

3 | Finding the most similar pair

Example

Underline the pair of words most similar in meaning.

come, go   roams, wanders   fear, fare

price / cost of travel
word for food / cooking.

How to do it

Look at each pair closely, saying the words in your head, working from left to right. Consider how the two words in each pair are related.

Check what relationship is being asked for in the question. This question type is asking for 'most similar in meaning'.

Start here
▼
come, go   *these are opposites*

roams, wanders   *these are very similar in meaning*

Underline <u>roams</u>, <u>wanders</u>. Scan the last pair.

fear, fare   *these are very similar in spelling and sound but not in meaning*

So your selected answer is correct.

Now try these

Underline the pair of words most similar in meaning.

1 hot, cold	tea, coffee	<u>dish, bowl</u>	
2 paint, brush	<u>melody, tune</u>	drum, noise	
3 <u>jog, trot</u>	run, fast	ramble, countryside	
4 hill, valley	<u>meadow, pasture</u>	summer, winter	

4 Choosing the best word to go with a given word

Underline the one word in the brackets closest in meaning to the word outside the brackets.

unhappy   (unkind, death, laughter, sad, friendly)

How to do it

Check the word 'unhappy' against each of the words inside the brackets in turn.
Work along the line of words in order, from left to right.
Remember you are looking for the word closest in meaning.

Start here

unhappy   (unkind, death, laughter, sad, friendly)

unhappy – unkind   *similar or same meaning?* **No**
    ! Sometimes linked together, but not same meaning

unhappy – death   *similar or same meaning?* **No**

unhappy – laughter   *similar or same meaning?* **No**
    ! These are associated with opposite emotions

unhappy – sad   *similar or same meaning?* **Yes**

Underline **sad**.

Scan any remaining words.

unhappy – friendly   *similar or same meaning?* **No**

So your selected answer is correct.

Now try these

Underline the one word in the brackets closest in meaning to the word outside the brackets.

1 start   (stop, finish, continue, commence, green)

2 hit   (bump, chart, thump, hard, run)

3 spring   (wire, autumn, blossom, pounce, rain)

4 shore   (boat, coast, shell, holiday, lighthouse)

5 | Choosing words to make a similar pair

Underline the two words, one from each group, which are closest in meaning.

(race, shop, start)   (finish, begin, end)

How to do it

Check the first word in the first group against each word in the second group in turn. Repeat with the second word in the first group and then with the third word from the first group, until you find the answer.

Start here

(race, shop, start)   (finish, begin, end)
  1st 2nd 3rd   *1st   2nd   3rd*

race – finish	*same meaning?*	**No**
race – begin	*same meaning?*	**No**
race – end	*same meaning?*	**No**

Many of the words given are related or used together – but they do not have the same meaning!

No answer yet, so repeat the process using the second word from the first set of brackets.

shop – finish	*same meaning?*	**No**
shop – begin	*same meaning?*	**No**
shop – end	*same meaning?*	**No**

No answer yet, so repeat the process using the third word from the first set of brackets.

start – finish	*same meaning?*	**No**, *opposites*
start – begin	*same meaning?*	**Yes**

Underline both words, **start** and **begin**.

Scan the last option.

start – end	*same meaning?*	**No**, *opposites*

So the selected pair is the correct answer.

Now try these

Underline the two words, one from each group, which are closest in meaning.

1 (brother, friend, animal)   (family, horse, chum)

2 (mouse, red, berries)   (cheese, black, scarlet)

3 (building, crane, shed)   (scaffolding, hut, skyscraper)

4 (arch, canopy, umbrella)   (cave, storm, awning)

Underline the two words which are the odd ones out in the following group of words.

black　　　king　　　purple　　　green　　　house

How to do it

Read each word carefully, from left to right, saying it in your head.
Think about what group or groups of things each word could belong to; it is usually quite clear. Find which three belong to a common group and underline the odd ones out.

Start here
▼

black　　　*colour*, *dark*, *opposite of white*

　　　king　　　*person, leader, royal*

　　　　　purple　　　*colour*, *lilac*, *flowers*

　　　　　　　green　　　*colour*, *grass*, (*jealousy*, *environmentally friendly*)

　　　　　　　　　house　　　*building*, *home*

Clearly, three are colours, so underline <u>**king**</u> and <u>**house**</u> as they are the odd ones out.

Now try these

Underline the two words which are the odd ones out in the following groups of words.

1. house　　　office　　　<u>tractor</u>　　　bungalow　　　<u>chimney</u>
2. bread　　　biscuits　　　<u>picnic</u>　　　<u>knife</u>　　　cake
3. opera　　　sitcom　　　<u>compass</u>　　　concert　　　<u>palace</u>
4. dinghy　　　<u>horse</u>　　　yacht　　　canoe　　　<u>bicycle</u>

Example

Underline the two words from the group below which are most similar in type or meaning.

dear   pleasant   poor   extravagant   expensive

How to do it

Read the first word on the left – remember to say it in your head.
Then, thinking of its meaning and associations, compare it with each of the other words in that line in turn.
Repeat the process starting with the second word.
You only need to compare this word with the words on the right of it.

Start here
▼
dear   *friend, precious, costly*

dear – pleasant   *similar?*   **No**

dear – poor   *similar?*   **No**

dear – extravagant   *similar?*   **No**

dear – expensive   *similar?*   **Yes**

Underline the words __dear__ and __expensive__.

Scan the remaining words to check that there are no other obvious options.

Now try these

Underline the two words in each line which are most similar in type or meaning.

1 pineapple   duck   book   banana   edible

2 carriage   horse   field   straw   pony

3 sparkle   tinsel   glass   twinkle   cake

4 soldier   battle   brave   courageous   tank

8 Choosing one word to go with the given set of words

Underline the word in the brackets which goes best with the words given outside the brackets.

word, paragraph, sentence   (pen, cap, letter, top, stop)

How to do it

Carefully read the words given outside the brackets. Identify what they have in common, or what they are all to do with. Then read each of the words in the brackets in turn, from left to right, saying them in your head and checking them against the set outside the brackets.

Start here
▼

word, paragraph, sentence	*these are all to do with writing, the elements that make up a piece of writing*
pen?	*not really – a tool used for writing but not an element of writing. Is there anything better?*
cap?	**No**, *not connected*
letter?	**Yes**, *paragraphs are made up of sentences, which are made up of words, which are made up of letters*

Underline the word <u>letter</u>.

Scan the remaining words to check that there are no other obvious options.

top?	**No**
stop?	**No** – *reminds you of a 'full stop' in punctuation, but 'stop' alone is not an element of writing*

Now try these

Underline the word in the brackets which goes best with the words given outside the brackets.

1 monitor, hard-drive, keyboard   (pen, <u>mouse</u>, cat, paper, piano)

2 milk, butter, cheese   (potato, cow, bread, <u>yoghurt</u>, breakfast)

3 rain, snow, drizzle   (grey, winter, <u>hail</u>, anorak, skiing)

4 quaver, rest, stave   (bench, <u>minim</u>, orchestra, festival, production)

9 | Finding a word similar in meaning

Example

Find a word that is similar in meaning to the word in capital letters and that rhymes with the second word.

CABLE   Tyre   _____

How to do it

Read both words saying them in your head.
Think about the meaning of the first word and the sound of the second word.
Then, looking at 'CABLE', start saying in your head words that rhyme with 'tyre'.
From these options write down the one most similar in meaning to 'CABLE'.

Start here
▼
CABLE   Tyre

CABLE		*tyre?*	**No**
		higher?	**No**
		fire?	**No**
		wire?	**Yes**

Write in the word <u>wire</u>.

Now try these

Find a word that is similar in meaning to the word given in capital letters and that rhymes with the second word.

1 TREK   Bike   _____

2 LANTERN   Camp   _____

3 SLUMBER   Weep   _____

4 GRIEF   Borrow   _____

10 Choosing the word most opposite to the given word

Underline one word from those in the brackets which is opposite in meaning to the word outside the brackets.

wide   (broad, vague, long, narrow, motorway)

How to do it

Check the word 'wide' against each of the words inside the brackets.
Work along the line of words in order, starting on the left.
Remember you are looking for **opposites**.

Start here
▼

wide   (broad, vague, long, narrow, motorway)

wide – broad	*opposites?*	**No**, *these are similar*
wide – vague	*opposites?*	**No**
wide – long	*opposites?*	**No**
wide – narrow	*opposites?*	**Yes**

Underline <u>narrow</u> and scan the remaining words to check that there are no other better options.

wide – motorway   *opposites?*   **No**

Now try these

Underline one word from those in the brackets which is opposite in meaning to the word outside the brackets.

1 reliable   (good, relation, untrustworthy, friend, bad)

2 healthy   (strong, energetic, medicine, ill, hospital)

3 diluted   (watered, cocktail, concentrated, cordial, drink)

4 kind   (generous, dishonest, lazy, thoughtful, cruel)

11 Choosing the pair of opposites

Underline the pair of words opposite in meaning.

cup, mug   coffee, milk   hot, cold

How to do it

Read each pair of words carefully saying them in your head.
Consider how the two words are connected, if at all.
Are they opposites?

Start here
▼

cup, mug	*similar objects*	*opposites?*	**No**
coffee, milk	*different drinks*	*opposites?*	**No**
hot, cold	*describing words*	*opposites?*	**Yes**

Underline <u>hot</u>, <u>cold</u>.

Remember to scan the remaining options if you find the answer before reaching the last choice.

Now try these

Underline the pair of words opposite in meaning.

1 halt, stop   broad, wide   cheap, expensive

2 rude, insolent   courteous, polite   considerate, thoughtless

3 accident, fire   dangerous, safe   emergency, police

4 descend, ascend   escalator, lift   stairs, carpet

12 Choosing the two opposite words

Underline the two words, one from each group, which are opposite in meaning.

(dawn, early, wake)   (late, stop, sunrise)

How to do it

Check the first word in the first group against each word in the second group in turn, working from left to right. Repeat the process with the second word from the first group, and then with the third word from the first group, until you find the answer.

Start here

(dawn, early, wake)   (late, stop, sunrise)
1st   2nd   3rd   *1st   2nd   3rd*

dawn – late		*opposites?*	**No**, *dawn and late may seem to suggest opposite things but they are not true opposites.*
dawn – stop		*opposites?*	**No**
dawn – sunrise		*opposites?*	**No**, *these are similar*

Now start with the second word from the first set of brackets.

early – late   *opposites?*   **Yes**

Underline **early** and **late**.

Scan the remaining words to check that there are no better options.

Now try these

Underline the two words, one from each group, which are opposite in meaning.

1 (fat, short, slim)   (strong, heavy, tall)

2 (discover, find, treasure)   (lose, trail, map)

3 (aunt, old, cousin)   (relations, family, young)

4 (reduce, sale, market)   (bargain, increase, shopping)

13 Choosing a word to go with two pairs of words

Underline the one word in the brackets which will go equally well with both the pairs of words outside the brackets.

rush, attack   cost, fee   (price, hasten, strike, charge, money)

How to do it

Look at each pair of words in turn, saying the words in your head and thinking about how they are similar to each other.
Then consider each of the words in the brackets in turn, working from left to right.
Saying the word in your head, look at the two pairs of words in turn.
Is it similar to the first pair of words? Is it similar to the second pair of words?
Remember the word must be similar to both pairs of words to be correct.

Start here

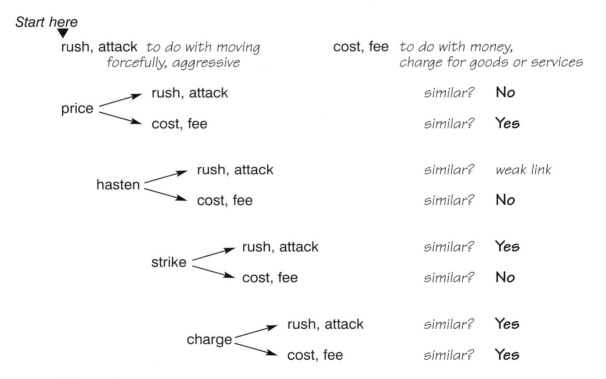

'Charge' is similar in meaning to both 'rush' and 'attack', and 'cost' and 'fee', so underline *charge*.

Scan the remaining word to check that there are no better options.

Now try these

Underline the one word in the brackets which will go equally well with both the pairs of words outside the brackets.

1 world, planet   soil, ground   (night, space, earth, garden, sphere)

2 rails, tracks   script, parts   (trains, play, electric, lines, cable)

3 club, heart   emerald, ruby   (garden, diamond, heart, forever, ring)

4 swan, goose   dip, dodge   (coot, water, avoid, feathers, duck)

14 Finding a three letter word to complete a longer word

Example

Find the three letter word which can be added to the letters in capitals to make a new word. The new word will complete the sentence sensibly. Write the three letter word.

The cat sprang onto the MO. _USE_

How to do it

Read the sentence carefully, saying it in your head, leaving a blank where the new word will go. Consider which words could complete the sentence sensibly. Match the words to the letters given. The correct answer will give a proper three letter word.

Start here
▼

The cat sprang onto the _____ *BIRD?*

CHEESE?

MOUSE?

'MOUSE' is the option which contains the two given letters 'M' and 'O'.
Removing the 'M' and 'O' leaves '<u>USE</u>' – a three letter word, so that is the answer.

Now try these

Find the three letter word which can be added to the letters in capitals to make a new word. The new word will complete the sentence sensibly. Write the three letter word.

1 The THRE was packed for the first performance. _EAT_

2 She took a POGRAPH of the splendid view. _HOT_

3 The artist's work was in the EXHIION. _BIT_

4 The planes CRED into the sea. _ASH_

22

15 Finding a letter to end one word and start another

Find the letter which will end the first word and start the second word.

d r o w (n) o u g h t

How to do it

Look at the first incomplete word and sound it out in your head.
Think of words which start with that sound, completing them in your head.
For each option check these points: Is it a proper word?
                                               Is it spelt correctly?
                                               Is it completed by adding just one letter?
When the answer is 'Yes' to each of these check questions, try the letter in front of the second incomplete word.

Start here
▼

drowsy   *proper word?* **Yes**
                      spelt correctly? **Yes**
                      one letter added? **No**

       drowt   *proper word?* *Sounds correct*
                      spelt correctly? **No**, *should be 'drought'*

         drown   *proper word?* **Yes**
                      spelt correctly? **Yes**
                      one letter added? **Yes**

The answers are all 'Yes', so try the letter in front of the second incomplete word. Does it make a proper word?

n   o u g h t   nought   **Yes**

The correct answer is the letter '**n**'.

If you have difficulty thinking of possible words from sounding out the incomplete word given, work quickly and methodically through the letters of the alphabet, you will soon identify some options. Check these options in the same way as shown above.
If you have no luck with the first word, try working with the second word.

Now try these

Find the letter which will end the first word and start the second word.

    1 p e a c (*h*) o m e

    2 w i n (*d*) a r k

    3 s h o v e (*l*) e a v e r

    4 s p a r (*k*) n i g h t

Variations

Variations of this question type include finding two letters to complete the first word and start the second. The method is the same but the third check question is adapted:

    Is it a proper word?
    Is it spelt correctly?
    Is it completed with the addition of two letters?

Now try these

Find the two letters which will end the first word and start the second word.

    5 r e a (*ch*) a i r

    6 w a (_ _) o o n

    7 b r a c k (_ _) t i c e

    8 d a m a (_ _) n t l e

dama

16 | Finding letters to complete two pairs of words

Example

Find the letter which will complete both pairs of words, ending the first word and starting the second. The same letter must be used for both pairs of words.

m e a (__) a b l e   f i (__) u b

How to do it

The method is the same as for question type 15 with an additional final stage. Look at the first, incomplete word and sound it out in your head.

Think of words which start with that sound, completing them in your head.

For each option check: Is it a proper word? Is it spelt correctly? Is it completed by adding just one letter?

When the answer is 'Yes' to each of these check questions, try the letter in front of the second incomplete word.

If that is a proper word, then check the letter in the second pair of incomplete words.

Start here
▼
mea__

meal   *proper word?*   **Yes**
        spelt correctly?   **Yes**
        one letter added?   **Yes**
   Try 'l' in front of the second incomplete word.
   l   a b l e   lable   **No**, *sounds like a proper word but spelt incorrectly.*

     mean   *proper word?*   **Yes**
            spelt correctly?   **Yes**
            one letter added?   **Yes**
    Try 'n' in front of the second incomplete word.
    n   a b l e   nable   **No**, *not a proper word*

        meat   *proper word?*   **Yes**
                spelt correctly?   **Yes**
                one letter added?   **Yes**
     Try 't' in front of the second incomplete word.
     t   a b l e   table   **Yes**

Now try 't' in the second pair of incomplete words.
           f i   t   fit   **Yes**
           t   u b   tub   **Yes**

   The correct answer is the letter '<u>t</u>'.

If you have difficulty thinking of possible words from sounding out the incomplete word given, work quickly and methodically through the letters of the alphabet, you will soon identify some options. Check these options in the same way as shown above.

If you have no luck with the first word, try working with the second word.

Now try these

Find the letter which will complete both pairs of words, ending the first word and starting the second. The same letter must be used for both pairs of words.

1 b o o (__) o o l   b o a (__) u n e   **2** r e a (__) u s t   b o n (__) o n k e y

3 c l a s (__) u n t   j u m (__) o l a r   **4** w i l l o (__) a n d   j a (__) a k e

Variation

Some questions require two letters to be found. The letters together will complete both pairs of words, ending the first word and starting the second.

> **Example**
>
> b e a (__ __) r a p   c o a (__ __) i n g

How to do it

The same method applies, but after thinking of words which start with that sound and completing them in your head, check: Is it a proper word?

                                         Is it spelt correctly?

                                         Is it completed with the addition of two letters?

When the answer is 'Yes' to each of these check questions, try the letters in front of the second incomplete word. If that is a proper word, check it with the second pair of words. As before, if you have no luck with the first pair of words try the second.

Start here
▼

bea __ __   beard   *proper word?*   **Yes**

                             spelt correctly?   **Yes**

                             two letters added?   **Yes**

Try 'r d' in front of the second incomplete word.

         r d   r a p   rdrap   **No**, *not a proper word*

                 beast   *proper word?*   **Yes**

                             spelt correctly?   **Yes**

                             two letters added?   **Yes**

Try 's t' in front of the second incomplete word.

         s t   r a p   strap   **Yes**, *a proper word*

Now try 's t' in the second pair of incomplete words.

         c o a   s t   coast   **Yes**

         s t   i n g   sting   **Yes**

The correct answer is '<u>st</u>'.

Now try these

5 b e n (__ __) a r t   b r a n (__ __) a i n

6 w i d (__ __) r o n e   e a r (__ __) i s t l e

7 c h o s (__ __) g a g e   f a s t (__ __) t r a n c e

8 m a s t (__ __) r o r s   w e a t h (__ __) u p t

17 | Sorting letters to give a proper word

Rearrange the muddled letters in capitals to make a proper word. The answer will complete the sentence sensibly.

A BEZAR is an animal with stripes. _____

How to do it

Read the sentence carefully saying the words in your head and leaving a blank in the place of the jumbled up word.

The clue will suggest certain possible answers, consider each in turn and compare them to the letters given. Keep the letters in mind while thinking up possible words.

Start here
▼
BEZAR

A _____ is an animal with stripes.

Tiger?	A tiger is an animal with stripes.	*Does it make sense?*	**Yes**
		Same letters?	**No**
Badger?	A badger is an animal with stripes.	*Does it make sense?*	**Yes**
		Same letters?	**No**
Zebra?	A zebra is an animal with stripes.	*Does it make sense?*	**Yes**
		Same letters?	**Yes**

ZEBRA is the correct answer so write it in.

Now try these

Rearrange the muddled letters in capitals to make a proper word. The answer will complete the sentence sensibly.

1 A NEPLPIPAE is a sweet tropical fruit. _____

2 A LANCA is a manmade waterway. _____

3 CREDADH is a type of cheese. _____

4 A GYCENT is a young swan. _____

18 Sorting letters into words to complete the sentence

Example

Rearrange the muddled words in capital letters in the following sentence so that it makes sense.

There are sixty SNODCES _____ in a UTMINE _____ .

How to do it

Read the sentence through, saying the words in your head and replacing the jumbled words with 'somethings' or 'something'.
Using the clues in the sentence consider possible options for the first word.
Test them out. The correct word will suggest possible options for the second word.

Start here
▼

There are sixty 'somethings' in a 'something'.

Clue: sixty *therefore not metric measures*
could be related to time
sixty minutes?
There are sixty **minutes** in an **hour**.

Correct sentence but 'minutes' does not match the given letters 'SNODCES'.

sixty seconds?
There are sixty **seconds** in a **minute**.

Correct sentence, which matches the given letters.

Fill in the missing words, <u>**seconds**</u> and <u>**minute**</u>.

If you have difficulty with the first word go on to the second word.

Now try these

Rearrange the muddled words in capital letters in the following sentences so that they make sense.

1 There are NEEVS _____ days in a KEWE _____ .

2 SKEANS _____ and DRIZALS _____ are reptiles.

3 There are twenty-six TRETELS _____ in the PABATHEL _____ .

4 STREVEE _____ is in the HAILYAMA _____ mountains.

28

19 Finding the odd one out by matching letters

Example

Underline the one word in each group which cannot be made from the letters of the word in capital letters.

STATIONERY   stone   tyres   ration   nation   noisy

How to do it

These questions are working at the letter level.

Look at the first word very carefully, letter by letter, checking that each one is present in the word 'STATIONERY'. (Notice that from this word you could have two 'T's but only one of each of the other letters.)

Continue working along the words from left to right until you find the word which contains a letter not available from the word 'STATIONERY' and underline it.

Start here
▼

STATIONERY	stone	*all letters available?* **Yes**
	tyres	*all letters available?* **Yes**
	ration	*all letters available?* **Yes**
	nation	*all letters available?* **No,** *there is only one 'n'*

So underline the word **nation**. Check the word 'noisy' just to be sure.

Now try these

Underline the one word in each group which **cannot** be made from the letters of the word in capital letters.

1 CORPORATION	troop	actor	notice	train	oration
2 ORCHESTRA	reach	chest	stretch	torch	crate
3 UNIVERSITY	tune	unity	strive	ruin	verse
4 PERIMETER	prime	tripe	timer	metric	merit

20 Choosing a word with letters in common

Example

Underline the one word which can be made from the letters of the word in capital letters.

CHAMPION   camping   notch   peach   cramp   chimp

How to do it

These questions are working at the letter level.
Look at the first word very carefully, letter by letter, checking to see if each letter is present in the word 'CHAMPION'.
Continue working along the words from left to right until you find the word which only contains letters present in the word 'CHAMPION' and underline it.

Start here
▼

CHAMPION	camping	*all letters available?* **No,** *there is no 'g'*
	notch	*all letters available?* **No,** *there is no 't'*
	peach	*all letters available?* **No,** *there is no 'e'*
	cramp	*all letters available?* **No,** *there is no 'r'*
	chimp	*all letters available?* **Yes**

Underline the word <u>*chimp*</u>.

Now try these

Underline the one word which **can be made** from the letters of the word in capital letters on the left.

1	MOUNTAIN	town	meant	none	tomb	main
2	TREASURE	street	stair	stream	stand	arrest
3	BREAKFAST	frost	fasten	stroke	streak	fresh
4	GEOGRAPHY	pages	hyphen	opera	grange	rough

21 Finding the odd one out by using a given rule

Example

Which one of the following words contains only the first six letters of the alphabet?

defeat   farce   abide   deaf   dice

How to do it

First of all you need to write down the letters that can be used, ie the first six letters of the alphabet.

1st	2nd	3rd	4th	5th	6th
a	b	c	d	e	f

Beginning with the first word on the left, match it letter by letter with these six letters.
Repeat the process with the other words.
Underline the word which can be made from the given six letters.

Start here
▼

First 6 letters of alphabet: a b c d e f

defeat   *all letters available?*
                No, *there is no letter 't'*

    farce   *all letters available?*
                No, *there is no letter 'r'*

      abide   *all letters available?*
                No, *there is no letter 'i'*

        deaf   *all letters available?*
                Yes

Underline the word *dea*f.

          dice   *all letters available?*
                No, *there is no letter 'i'*

So your selected answer is correct.

Now try these

In each line, which one word contains only the first six letters of the alphabet?

1	fast	feed	fare	fear	feet	_____
2	back	bend	bead	beach	bread	_____
3	daft	dare	dead	deal	dice	_____
4	barb	beard	bean	beef	band	_____

Choosing two words made from the same letters

Underline the two words which are made from the same letters.

tap   pet   tea   pot   eat

How to do it

These questions are working at the letter level. The letters in each word have to be compared with those of the other words.

Start with the word on the left and compare its letters with those of each of the other words in turn. Then look at the second word and compare its letters with those of each word to its right. Repeat the process until you find two words with the same letters.

You do not need to compare a word with the words on its left as they have already been compared.

Start here

tap   pet   tea   pot   eat

tap	pet				*same letters?* **No**
		tea			*same letters?* **No**
			pot		*same letters?* **No**
				eat	*same letters?* **No**
	pet	tea			*same letters?* **No**
			pot		*same letters?* **No**
				eat	*same letters?* **No**
		tea	pot		*same letters?* **No**
				eat	*same letters?* **Yes**

Underline <u>*tea*</u> and <u>*eat*</u>.

Now try these

Underline the two words which are made from the same letters.

1 seat   state   rates   trait   rats   eats

2 peach   each   cheer   chap   arch   ache

3 field   filled   friend   flier   filed   felled

4 poster stopper porter   spotter report strop

23 | Choosing two words that go together to make one new word

Underline two words, one from each group, that go together to form a new word. The word in the first group always comes first.

    (hand, green, for)   (light, house, sure)

How to do it

Each word in the first set of brackets must be tested in front of each word in the second set of brackets. The words need to be said in your head to check whether they form a new word.

Start here
▼

hand – light	*does this form a new word?*	**No**
hand – house	*does this form a new word?*	**No**
hand – sure	*does this form a new word?*	**No**
green – light	*does this form a new word?*	**No,** *can go together but not one word*
green – house	*does this form a new word?*	**Yes,** *'greenhouse', a proper word, spelt correctly*

Underline <u>green</u> and <u>house</u>, and check the remaining possibilities just in case there is a better option.

Now try these

Underline two words, one from each group, that go together to form a new word. The word in the first group always comes first.

1 (light, hot, sun)   (sun, shine, summer)

2 (mat, test, green)   (fog, house, horn)

3 (face, cream, hand)   (paste, some, left)

4 (tall, ship, slip)   (gang, stock, way)

24 Making a new set of words by finding a single word prefix

Find a word that can be put in front of each of the following words to make a new, compound word.

cast   fall   ward   pour   _____

How to do it

These questions require you to come up with lots of ideas which you then test out.
You have to have a 'brain storm'. Starting with the first word on the left, think of as many different compound words as you can which are '_____cast'. Then test each of these prefixes against the other words, working from left to right.

Start here
▼

cast	overcast	*overfall?*	No
	forecast	*forefall?*	No
	downcast	*downfall?*	Yes
		downward?	Yes
		downpour?	Yes

The word 'down' can be added in front of each word, giving four proper new words, so the answer is **_down_**.

If you had not thought of 'downcast', move on from '_____cast' to '_____fall' and repeat the process.

Now try these

Find a word that can be put in front of each of the following words to make a new, compound word.

1 colour   cress   proof   fall   _____

2 card   code   age   script   _____

3 cup   fly   milk   scotch   _____

4 day   set   burn   shine   _____

Finding the hidden four letter word in a sentence

Write the four letter word hidden at the end of one word and the beginning of the next word in this sentence. The order of the letters may not be changed.

    We had bats and balls.   _____

How to do it

To do this type of question begin with the first word of the sentence and count along four letters.
If the four letters do not bridge a gap between words, ignore them.
If the four letters cross a gap between two words, look carefully to see if they make a proper, four letter word.
Continue working along the sentence until you find the word.

Start here
▼
   We had bats and balls.

W e h a	*across a gap?*	**Yes**	*a word?*	**No**
e h a d	*across a gap?*	**Yes**	*a word?*	**No**
h a d b	*across a gap?*	**Yes**	*a word?*	**No**
a d b a	*across a gap?*	**Yes**	*a word?*	**No**
d b a t	*across a gap?*	**Yes**	*a word?*	**No**
b a t s	*across a gap?*	**No**		
a t s a	*across a gap?*	**Yes**	*a word?*	**No**
t s a n	*across a gap?*	**Yes**	*a word?*	**No**
s a n d	*across a gap ?*	**Yes**	*a word?*	**Yes**

The four letter word is <u>sand</u>.

Continue to look for other options.

Now try these

Write the four letter word hidden at the end of one word and the beginning of the next word in each sentence. The order of the letters may not be changed.

1 She went to the car empty handed.   _____

2 Who leant on my bike?   _____

3 I will come at ten o'clock.   _____

4 The round tin was open.   _____

26 Making new words by changing one letter at a time

Example

Change the first word into the last word by changing one letter at a time and making a new, different word in the middle.

CASE _____ LASH

How to do it

Look carefully at the first and last words, noticing which letters stay the same.
The middle word is made from changing either of the other letters (the 'C' to the 'L', or the 'E' to the 'H') so try these changes in turn.

Start here
▼
CASE _____ LASH

Which letters stay the same?   **A** and **S**

So try changing the others:

C to L	gives LASE	*is this a proper word?*	**No**
E to H	gives CASH	*is this a proper word?*	**Yes**

<u>CASH</u> is the answer.

Now try these

Change the first word into the last word by changing one letter at a time and making a new, different word in the middle.

1 LAND _____ LAME

2 COLD _____ HOLE

3 FIRE _____ FIND

4 SHOE _____ SLOW

Variation

Change the first word into the last word by changing one letter at a time and making two new, different words in the middle.

PEAS _____ _____ RENT

Start here
▼
PEAS _____ _____ RENT

Which letter stays the same? **E**

Then try changing the other letters in turn, starting from the left.

P to R	gives	REAS	*is this a proper word?*	**No**
A to N	gives	PENS	*is this a proper word?*	**Yes**
P to R	gives	RENS	*is this a proper word?*	**No** *(sounds correct but not spelt correctly)*
S to T	gives	PENT	*is this a proper word?*	**Yes**
P to R	gives	RENT	*this is the final word*	

So the answer is: PEAS <u>PENS</u> <u>PENT</u> RENT

Note that there may be more than one correct answer with questions of this type. The above would also be correct as:

PEAS <u>PEAT</u> <u>PENT</u> RENT

Now try these

Change the first word into the last word by changing one letter at a time and making two new, different words in the middle.

5 MULE _____ _____ SILK

6 TENT _____ _____ PAST

7 WHEN _____ _____ THAT

8 BOLT _____ _____ FELL

Finding a pattern then completing the last pair of words

Change the first word of the third pair in the same way as the other pairs to give a new word.

bind, hind   bare, hare   but, _____

How to do it

Look carefully at the first pair of words.
How is the second word different from the first word?
If there is more than one possible answer try out each option in turn.
Considering one of the ways in which the two words are different, check it against the second pair of words. Are they also different in the same way?
If yes, apply the difference to the third pair to find the last word.
If no, try one of the other options.

Start here
▼

bind, hind   *the 'b' in the first word changes to an 'h' in the second word*

bare, hare   *here also the 'b' in the first word changes to an 'h'*

try changing the '**b**' to an '**h**' in the third pair:

but   **hut**   *is the new word a proper word?*
Yes

The answer is <u>hut</u>.

Now try these

Change the first word of the third pair in the same way as the other pairs to give a new word.

1 lad, land   bad, band   sad, _____

2 four, flour   bow, blow   sower, _____

3 fat, fate   wan, wane   pan, _____

4 prose, rose   stake, take   brook, _____

28 Making two new words by transferring one letter

Example

Move one letter from the first word to the second word to make two new words.

hunt   sip   _____   _____

How to do it

Look carefully at the letters within the first word. Working from left to right, remove each letter in turn from the word to check whether the remaining letters form a proper word.
If they do then try adding that letter to the second word, working from left to right and considering each possible position in turn.
Remember the letter could be added right at the beginning of the word or at any position within it.

Start here
▼

hunt   u n t   *proper word?* **No**

h̶u̶n t   h n t   *proper word?* **No**

h u ̶n̶t   h u t   *proper word?* **Yes**   *The letter removed is an 'n'*

Now try adding an 'n' to each position in the second word to make a new word:

↑	s	↑	i	↑	p	↑
1st position		*2nd position*		*3rd position*		*4th position*

1st option   n s i p   *proper word?* **No**

2nd option   s n i p   *proper word?* **Yes**

So the answer is <u>hut</u> and <u>snip</u>.

Now try these

Move one letter from the first word to the second word to make two new words.

1 scan   end   _____   _____

2 plaice   sad   _____   _____

3 stray   lowly   _____   _____

4 crease   sting   _____   _____

40

Making a new set of words by prefixing one letter

Which one letter can be added to the front of all of these words to make new words?

    __are   __at   __rate   __all

How to do it

Looking at the first word on the left, go through the alphabet mentally adding each letter in turn onto the front. When one of the letters makes a proper word, test that same letter in front of the other words in turn, working from left to right. The letter which, when added to the front, makes new words with all of the words in the line is the correct answer.

Start here
▼

a-are   *proper word?* **No**

      b-are   *proper word?* **Yes,** *so check it against the other words*

          b-at   *proper word?* **Yes**

             b-rate   *proper word?* **No,** *so continue with trying the next letter in the alphabet starting again with the first word*

c-are   *proper word?* **Yes,** *so check it against the other words*

      c-at   *proper word?* **Yes**

          c-rate   *proper word?* **Yes**

             c-all   *proper word?* **Yes**

So the correct answer is the letter '*c*'.

Now try these

Which one letter can be added to the front of all of these words to make new words?

1 __air   __are   __ear   __lop   __lute

2 __and   __lay   __top   __tone   __oak

3 __ail   __lease   __eat   __reach   __late

4 __hen   __ail   __hat   __rite   __aft

30 Making a new word by adding one letter

Example

Add one letter to the word in capital letters to make a new word. The meaning of the new word is given in the clue.

PLAN   simple   _____

How to do it

There are two methods of tackling these question types. Look through both methods. Use the one which seems easier to you as your first option. Try the other method if you do not have any success with the first.

Method 1

Carefully read the clue and then brainstorm words similar in meaning which come to mind. Consider each of these words in turn, matching them with the word in capitals.
Do any of the options contain the same letters in the same order, with just one additional letter added? When the answer is 'Yes' you have found the correct word.

Start here
▼

simple	easy	*containing the letters P, L, A and N?* **No**, *try again*
	straightforward	*containing the letters P, L, A and N?* **No**, *try again*
	plain	*containing the letters P, L, A and N?* **Yes**. *has just one extra letter?* **Yes**

So the answer is <u>PLAIN</u>.

Method 2

Look carefully at the letters which make up the word in capitals.
Looking at the consonants, which of the single consonants or consonant blends could be made into a new blend by adding one letter? Check the new blends in the word. Do they make a proper word? If the answer is 'No', try again. If 'Yes', check the meaning of the new word fits with the clue.
If no single consonant can be added, consider the vowels. An additional vowel may form a new word by being added at the beginning of the word, at the end of the word or by forming a new vowel blend. Work through the vowels in order – a, e, i, o and u.

Start here
▼

PLAN Consonant blends

SPL	SPLAN	*a proper word?*	**No**
MPL	MPLAN	*a proper word?*	**No**
PPL	PPLAN	*a proper word?*	**No**
RPL	RPLAN	*a proper word?*	**No**

Options adding consonants to **PL** do not give any new words.

Try with the **N**.

PLA**N** Consonant blends

NC	PLANC	*a proper word?*	**No**
ND	PLAND	*a proper word?*	**No**
NG	PLANG	*a proper word?*	**No**
NK	PLANK	*a proper word?*	**Yes**
		means simple?	**No**
NS	PLANS	*a proper word?*	**Yes**
		means simple?	**No**
NT	PLANT	*a proper word?*	**Yes**
		means simple?	**No**

Options adding consonants to **N** do not give any new words.

Try the addition of **vowels**.

PLAN

A	APLAN	*a proper word?*	**No**
	PALAN	*a proper word?*	**No**
	PLAAN	*a proper word?*	**No**
	PLANA	*a proper word?*	**No**

PLAN

E	EPLAN	*a proper word?*	**No**
	PELAN	*a proper word?*	**No**
	PLEAN	*a proper word?*	**No**
	PLAEN	*a proper word?*	**No**
	PLANE	*a proper word?*	**Yes**
		means simple?	**No**

PLAN

I	IPLAN	*a proper word?*	**No**
	PILAN	*a proper word?*	**No**
	PLIAN	*a proper word?*	**No**
	PLAIN	*a proper word?*	**Yes**
		means simple?	**Yes**

So the answer is <u>PLAIN</u>.

Now try these

Add one letter to the word in capital letters to make a new word. The meaning of the new word is given in the clue.

1 CANE   a very tall, strong machine   _____

2 PEASANT   a long-tailed game bird   _____

3 LOWER   blossom   _____

4 PANTING   artist at work   _____

43

Example

Remove one letter from the word in capital letters to leave a new word. The meaning of the new word is given in the clue.

AUNT   an insect   _____

How to do it

Look carefully at the letters in the word given in capital letters, then remove each letter in turn, just one at a time and starting from the left. Do the remaining letters make a proper word? If they do, check the meaning of the word against the clue given. The word which matches the clue is the correct answer.

Start here
▼

A̶UNT	UNT	*a proper word?*	**No**
AU̶NT	ANT	*a proper word?*	**Yes**
		is an insect?	**Yes**

So the answer is <u>ANT</u>.

Now try these

Remove one letter from the word given in capital letters to leave a new word. The meaning of the new word is given in the clue.

1 SLANT   a thin strip of wood   _____

2 MONKEY   cash   _____

3 SPLICE   a piece of cake   _____

4 FLATTER   bigger   _____

32 Finding a pattern and making a new word in the same way

How to do it

Look carefully at the first group of three words. Notice what the middle word has in common with the first word, and what it has in common with the third word. Apply the same rule to the second group of words to make the new middle word.
Check that your answer is a proper, correctly spelt word.

Start here
▼

First triplet:

PAIN   **IN**TO   *the last 2 letters of the first word give the first 2 letters of the middle word*

          IN**TO** **TO**OK   *the first 2 letters of the last word give the last 2 letters of the middle word*

Now apply this rule to the second triplet:

Second triplet:

ALSO SO___
          ___ON ONLY

The new middle word is *SOON*.

Now try these

Look at the first group of three words. The word in the middle has been made from the other two words. Complete the second group of three words in the same way, making a new word in the middle of the group.

1 SEND ENDS SLUG   MICE _____ DONE

2 HOLE HATE BATS   FOLD _____ SEEN

3 MANY PONY POOL   PART _____ FOUR

4 HAND HAVE LIVE   DEBT _____ APED

33 Choosing the best word to complete a sentence

Complete the following sentence sensibly by selecting one word from each of the groups of words given in the brackets. Underline the words selected.

> The (fish, ant, dog) cut a (fin, leg, ball) in the (wind, water, fence).

How to do it

Scan the whole sentence as you might see the correct combination of words immediately. If you do, then reread the sentence very carefully thinking about what it means, and checking that it makes sense.

If you do not see a combination of words immediately, work carefully through each option in turn, always starting from the left. This may seem a lengthy process, but it is important to be methodical.

Start here
▼

The **fish** cut a *fin*	.....	*Does it make sense?* **Yes**
The **fish** cut a **fin** in the *wind?*		*Does it make sense?* **No**
The **fish** cut a **fin** in the *water?*		*Does it make sense ?* *Not really, fish and fins are in water, but fins don't get 'cut' in water.*
The **fish** cut a **fin** in the *fence?*		*Does it make sense?* **No**
The **fish** cut a *leg*	.....	*Fish do not have legs, so cannot make sense.*
The **fish** cut a *ball*	.....	*Fish don't play with balls, so cannot make sense.*
The **ant** cut a *fin*	.....	*Ants do not have fins, so cannot make sense.*
The **ant** cut a *leg*	.....	*Does it make sense?* **Yes**
The **ant** cut a **leg** in the *wind?*		*Does it make sense?* **No**, *ants have legs but legs don't get cut in wind.*
The **ant** cut a **leg** in the *water?*		*Does it make sense?* **No**, *ants have legs but legs do not get cut in water.*
The **ant** cut a **leg** in the *fence?*		*Does it make sense?* **No**, *ants' legs are too small to be cut by fences.*
The **ant** cut a *ball*	.....	*Ants do not play with balls, so cannot make sense.*
The **dog** cut a *fin*	.....	*Dogs do not have fins, so cannot make sense.*
The **dog** cut a *leg*	.....	*Does it make sense?* **Yes**
The **dog** cut a **leg** in the *wind?*		*Does it make sense?* **No**
The **dog** cut a **leg** in the *water?*		*Does it make sense?* **No**
The **dog** cut a **leg** in the *fence?*		*Does it make sense?* **Yes**

This sentence is the answer:

> The (fish, ant, <u>*dog*</u>) cut a (fin, <u>*leg*</u>, ball) in the (wind, water, <u>*fence*</u>).

Now try these

Complete the following sentence sensibly by selecting one word from each of the groups of words given in the brackets. Underline the words selected.

1 The (children, books, foxes) carried the (houses, books, steps) home from the (greengrocers, library, factory).

2 The (church, lady, flag) walked along the (clock, tower, path) to the (summer, castle, heart).

3 The (wind, girl, mouse) blew the (money, cheese, leaves) off the (wallet, clouds, trees).

4 The (bread, rain, sun) warmed the (seeds, night, clouds) in the (freezer, ground, chimney).

34 | Correcting sentences by changing the word order

Example

Find and underline the two words which need to change places for the sentence to make sense.

She went to letter the write.

How to do it

Read the sentence through twice – the first time read it really quickly, then reread it slowly and carefully. On the first quick read through you may automatically exchange the wrongly positioned words to make the sentence make sense. When reading slowly you will then see which two words are in the wrong places.

If you do not spot the wrongly placed words after reading through quickly, read through slowly and stop at the first word which appears to be wrong for the sentence to make sense. Then look at the remaining words, trying each in turn to see if they can be used to complete the sentence sensibly.

Start here
▼
She went to letter the write.

She went to letter ...   *at this point the sentence ceases to make sense.*

Use the remaining words to replace the word letter:

She went to the ...   *could be all right, continue ...*   letter write.   **No**

She went to the ...   write letter.   **No**

She went to write ...   *makes sense now, and clearly ends with ...*   the letter.

So underline the words <u>*letter*</u> and <u>*write*</u>.

Now try these

Find and underline the two words which need to change places for the sentence to make sense.

1 The morning fields shone brightly on the snowy sun.

2 The sun was melting in the ice-cream.

3 The family went for the seaside to the summer.

4 Every robin the day came into the garden.

48

35 Finding a pattern and choosing letters to complete in the same way

Example

Fill in the missing letters. The alphabet has been written out to help you.

A B C D E F G H I J K L M N O P Q R S T U V W X Y Z

AB is to CD   as   PQ is to ___

How to do it

Look carefully at the first two letters and locate them on the alphabet line.
Then locate the next two letters and notice the relationship between the two sets of letters which make up the first pair.
Having spotted a pattern or relationship locate the first two letters of the second pair on the alphabet line and then apply the rule to find the missing pair of letters.

Start here
▼
A B C D E F G H I J K L M N O P Q R S T U V W X Y Z

$\underbrace{\textbf{AB} \text{ is to } \text{CD}}_{First\ pair}$ as $\underbrace{\text{PQ is to } \_\_\_}_{Second\ pair}$

The second part of the pair is made up of the two consecutive letters after the first two.
Now apply this rule to the second pair.

A B C D E F G H I J K L M N O **P Q** R S T U V W X Y Z

$\underbrace{\text{AB is to } \text{CD}}_{First\ pair}$ as $\underbrace{\textbf{PQ} \text{ is to } \_\_\_}_{Second\ pair}$

So the missing letters are <u>RS</u>.

Now try these

Fill in the missing letters. The alphabet has been written out to help you.

A B C D E F G H I J K L M N O P Q R S T U V W X Y Z

1 DF is to EG   as   RT is to ___

2 KN is to QT   as   OR is to ___

3 AD is to BC   as   WZ is to ___

4 LK is to JI   as   SR is to ___

49

36 Finding a connection then choosing a word to complete a second pair in the same way

Example

Look at the pair of words on the left.

Underline one of the words in the brackets to go with the word outside the brackets in the same way as the first two words go together.

good, better   bad (naughty, worst, worse, nasty)

How to do it

Look carefully at the first pair of words and identify how they are related or connected.
Having found a link, test the same link on the second set of words.
Underline the selected word.
If there does not appear to be a corresponding word return to the first pair and try to find another link between them.

Start here
▼

good, better   bad (naughty, worst, worse, nasty)
1st pair of words   *2nd set of words*

Look carefully at the first pair of words:
     good is a positive word, meaning of high quality
     better is a comparative, one stage up on good

From this example it appears that the rule for the second word of the pair is that it is the comparative form of the first word, that is one stage up on it.
Try applying this rule to the second set of words.

     bad means poor or low quality, the comparative form of which is **worse**
         'worse' is one of the options available in the brackets

Underline *worse* as the correct answer.
Note it is not 'worst' because that is the superlative form, two stages up.

Now try these

Look at the pair of words on the left. Underline one of the words in the brackets to go with the word outside the brackets in the same way as the first two words go together.

1 stop, red   go (whistle, amber, start, green, move)

2 tall, short   wide (broad, fat, narrow, empty)

3 foot, feet   mouse (cheese, trap, vole, mice)

4 east, west   north (compass, south, bearings, north-west)

Finding a connection and completing the sentence by finding the missing word

Complete the following expressions by filling in the missing word.

Pen is to ink as brush is to _____ .

How to do it

Look carefully at the first part of the sentence which contains a pair of words from which you have to find the rule or relationship to apply to the second part of the sentence. Then find the equivalent word to complete the second part of the sentence.

Start here
▼
Pen is to ink …

The relationship is that the first uses the second.
The first applies the second.

Try applying this rule to the second part of the sentence.

… as brush is to … *not 'broom' because not looking for similarities*
not 'pan' because not looking for a pair of objects
could be 'hair'? But brush doesn't apply hair so continue to find a better option.
could be 'paint'? **Yes**, *brush uses and applies the paint*

Complete the whole sentence to check for sense:

Pen is to ink as brush is to **paint**.

Now try these

Complete the following expressions by filling in the missing word.

1 Cat is to kitten as swan is to _____ .

2 Artist is to pictures as composer is to _____ .

3 Stallion is to mare as boar is to _____ .

4 Light is to eye as sound is to _____ .

38 Choosing words to complete both expressions in the best way

Example

Complete the following sentences in the best way by choosing one word from each set of brackets.

Tall is to (tree, short, colour) as narrow is to (thin, white, wide).

How to do it

Look carefully at the first expression, completing it in your head with each of the three words in brackets in turn. One of the pairs will be related in a specific way, such as being similar in meaning, opposites or a natural pair.
Now apply the same relationship or rule to the second expression.
Read the word given, pairing it up with each of the words in the brackets in turn, working from left to right. The pair with the same relationship between them as the pair in the first expression is the correct response.
If there is no similar pair return to the first set and consider other relationships.

Start here

Tall is to (tree, short, colour) …

tall – tree   *a natural pair?* **Yes**, *but not unique, not all trees are tall*

tall – short   *a natural pair?* **Yes,** *opposites*

now look at the second part, looking for opposites

… as narrow is to (thin, white, wide).

narrow – thin   *opposites?* **No**, *they are similar*

narrow – white   *opposites?* **No**

narrow – wide   *opposites?* **Yes**

Then underline **short** and **wide** – these words are both opposites of the ones given.

Now try these

Complete the following sentences in the best way by choosing one word from each set of brackets.

1 Always is to (never, sometimes, free) as open is to (door, shut, ajar).

2 Poem is to (verse, rhymes, poet) as story is to (book, author, cover).

3 Car is to (tyres, petrol, road) as horse is to (cart, bridle-path, stable).

4 Caterpillar is to (cabbage, butterfly, summer) as tadpole is to (frog, pond, prince).

39 Choosing words to complete a second expression in the same way

Example

Choose two words, one from each set of brackets, to complete the sentence in the best way.

Smile is to happiness as (drink, tear, laugh) is to (whisper, laugh, sorrow).

How to do it

Look at the first expression carefully, reading it aloud in your head.
Notice how the two words within it are related.
Then work through the possible word pairings in the second expression, starting from the left.
Find the pair which shows the same relationship between them as the first.

Start here
▼

| Smile is to happiness | *happiness is a mood, state or feeling and smile is what you do in that state or how you show that feeling* |

as:

| drink is to whisper | *a natural pair?* **No** |

| drink is to laugh | *a natural pair?* **No** |

| drink is to sorrow | *a natural pair?* **No** |

| tear is to whisper | *a natural pair?* **No** |

| tear is to laugh | *a natural pair?* Could be*
They are opposites, but the relationship being looked for is an action that goes with or expresses a mood |

| tear is to sorrow | *a natural pair?* **Yes**
Sorrow is a state or mood of sadness and tears are linked with that state or an action which shows sorrow |

Read through the whole sentence with the selected words:

Smile is to happiness as tear is to sorrow.

Does it make sense? Yes
Underline the correct words for the answer:

Smile is to happiness as (drink, **_tear_**, laugh) is to (whisper, laugh, **_sorrow_**).

Now try these

Choose two words, one from each set of brackets, to complete the sentence in the best way.

1 Food is to hunger as (water, glass, drink) is to (famine, thirst, ice).

2 Apple is to orchard as (grape, France, wine) is to (plantation, vineyard, greenhouse).

3 Statue is to sculptor as (tower, building, design) is to (decorator, plan, architect).

4 Stream is to river as (pond, rain, flood) is to (winter, ocean, lake).

Crosswords

Example (1)

Fill in the crosswords so that all the missing words are included.

s	i	t

ivy, tee, eve, eye, see

How to do it

Start in the top left hand corner of the grid.
Find the word or words in the list which begin with the same letter in that corner – if there is just one word write it in.
If there are two options, consider each one in turn and notice which letters they would give to start the middle and bottom words going across the grid.
Are there words beginning with these letters? If yes, the word selected to go down from the top left hand corner may be correct. If not, then the word is not an option for the first word going down.
Continue with the third word down, comparing the last letters of the words across to check for correctness.
Next consider the middle word going down, or one of the two going across, choosing one which starts with a different letter from the other words. Only one option will be correct.
Put a line through each word as it is entered into the grid to check that none are omitted or repeated.

Start here
▼

s	i	t

ivy, tee, eve, eye, see

Which words begin with 's'?   only 'see'
so this word must be the first word going down
fill it in and cross it off

ivy, tee, eve, eye, ~~see~~

s	i	t
e		
e		

Which words begin with 't'?   only 'tee'
so this word must be the third word down
fill it in and cross it off

ivy, ~~tee~~, eve, eye, ~~see~~

s	i	t
e		e
e		e

The second word down begins with an 'i' whereas both the second and third words across begin with an 'e', so the next word which can be added is the second down, beginning with 'i', that is 'ivy'.

Fill it in and cross it off.   ~~ivy~~, ~~tee~~, eve, eye, ~~see~~

This completes the crossword.

s	i	t
e	v	e
e	y	e

Are the words 'eve' and 'eye' included? Check.
Yes, they are the second and third words across, respectively.

Now try these

Fill in the crosswords so that all the missing words are included.

1

t	a	t

too, tee, one, and, ode

2

		t
		e
		e

apt, pin, die, ado, one

56

3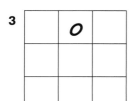

cap, ten, cot, pen, are, ore

4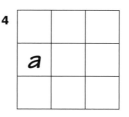

sip, ice, ten, sat, pen, ace

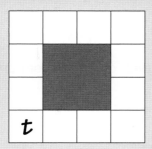

Example (2)

Fill in the crosswords so that all the missing words are included. You are given one letter from one of the words as a clue.

teas, tone, safe, tent

How to do it

Note the position of the letter written in the grid. Match this against the list of words. Fill in the word if there is only one option. Where there is more than one option check them in turn.

Start here
▼
The letter 't' given in the grid is the last letter of one word and the first of another. Three of the words start with 't' but only one ends with 't' so that word must be written in and crossed off the list.

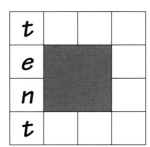

teas, tone, safe, ~~tent~~

Of the two words left beginning with 't', which one ends with the letter which starts the last word?　　　tea**s**

tone

The last word is 'safe', so 'teas' must go across the top of the grid.

t	e	a	s
e			a
n			f
t	o	n	e

Now try these

Fill in the crosswords so that all the words are included. You are given one letter from one of the words as a clue.

5

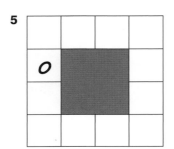

bead, tank, bolt, dark

6

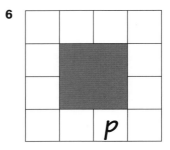

type, walk, kite, wait

7

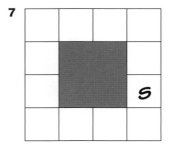

goal, each, lash, gate

8

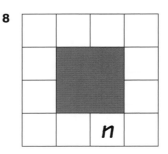

file, mint, form, east

58

Example (3)

patent, feeler, stoned, fasten, stolen, snored

How to do it

Count the position of the letter written in the grid. Match this against the list of words. Fill in the word if only one option. Where there is more than one option check them in turn.

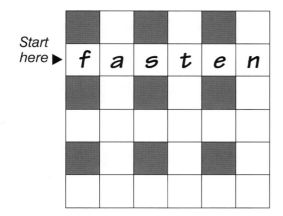

Start here ▶

The letter 's' given in the grid is the third letter in a word.
Which of the listed words has an 's' as its third letter? 'fasten'
Write in 'fasten', which then allows you to work out the next word.

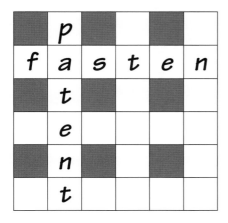

Cross the word 'fasten' off the list.
Which remaining word has 'a' as a second letter? 'patent'
Write it in and continue with the next word.

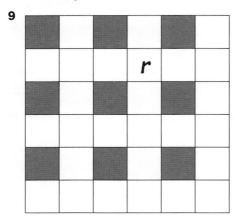

Cross the word 'patent' off the list.
Which remaining word has 'e' as a second letter?
'feeler'
Write it in and continue with the remaining words until complete.

Now try these

9

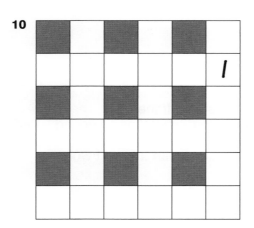

florin, snored, adored, skewer, drawer, flaked

10

closed, cutter, prided, stares, snored, tunnel

Finding a letter pattern and continuing the sequence

Example

Give the next two groups of letters in the following sequence.
The alphabet has been written out to help you.

A B C D E F G H I J K L M N O P Q R S T U V W X Y Z

CQ   DQ   EP   FP   ____   ____

How to do it

To do these question types you need to match up the given 'terms' or pairs of letters with the alphabet and spot a pattern in their order. Look carefully at the first letter of the first pair and then the second letter of the first pair. Note where they are on the alphabet line.
Then look carefully at the second pair. Where are they in relation to the first pair? Note the position and relationship. Then repeat with the following pairs. From the pattern you see, make up a rule which can then be applied to work out the missing letters needed to fill the gaps.

Start here   A B **C** D E F G H I J K L M N O P **Q** R S T U V W X Y Z
▼

CQ   DQ   *so far the first letter moves along one and the second*
1st pair 2nd pair   *letter of the pair stays the same*

Check this pattern with the 3rd and 4th pairs.

CQ   DQ   EP   FP
                    3rd pair 4th pair

does the first letter move one along the alphabet?
Yes
are the second letters the same as those of the first pair? **No**
are they the same as each other? **Yes**

The pattern could be: the first letter moves one along the alphabet each time
the second letter moves back one space along the alphabet, only changing every second pair

Apply this pattern to find out the next two letter pairs:

for the first letters C   D   E   F   **G**   **H**

for the second letters Q   Q   P   P   **O**   **O**

Now complete the gaps:

CQ   DQ   EP   FP   *GO*   *HO*

Give the next two groups of letters in the following sequence.
The alphabet has been written out to help you.

A B C D E F G H I J K L M N O P Q R S T U V W X Y Z

1 MO   KP   IQ   GR   ____   ____

2 AZ   CZ   EY   GY   ____   ____

3 GU   GV   HW   HX   ____   ____

4 MR   LS   KT   JU   ____   ____

Finding a number pattern and continuing the sequence

Example

Give the next two numbers in the following sequence.

a) simple sequence   2   4   6   8   __   __

b) complex sequence   5   21   8   17   11   13   __   __

How to do it

To continue any number sequence you need to establish the pattern.
Do this by looking at the differences between each term in the given sequence.
To find the differences you do a take away sum using the two numbers which are next to each other, taking the one on the left way from the one on the right. If the numbers are getting bigger the difference is positive (+) and if the numbers are getting smaller the difference is negative (−). To find out further terms of the sequence you just continue the pattern of differences.
If there is no regular pattern in the differences between each number, look at the differences between alternate numbers. Continue the pattern to work out the next numbers in the sequence.

Start here
▼

a) 2   4   6   8   __   __

       4 − 2?   *6 − 4?*   *8 − 6?*
       +2   *+2*   *+2*

The difference is always +2.
So by adding 2 to a term you can find the next term.
                                    8 + 2   **10**
                                           10 + 2   **12**

The answer is:
2   4   6   8   <u>10</u>   <u>12</u>

b)   5   21   8   17   11   13   __   __
Differences:
            +16   −13   +9   −6   +2

There is no regular pattern.
Try differences between alternate numbers.
When you find the correct pattern continue for the next two numbers.

Now try these

Give the next two numbers in the following sequences.

1 23   20   17   14   __   __

2 7   11   15   19   __   __

3 13   16   19   22   __   __

4 61   57   53   49   __   __

5 12   42   15   34   18   26   __   __

6 28   2   25   6   22   10   __   __

7 44   13   39   15   34   17   __   __

8 2   23   10   20   18   17   __   __

43 Placing words in alphabetical order

If these words are placed in alphabetical order, which word comes 4th in the list?

anxiety   auction   ancient   axiomatic   auxiliary

How to do it

When placing words in alphabetical order look carefully at the first letter in each word, then the second and then the third, etc.
Each time note down the one(s) which come(s) next.
(With questions which ask for the alphabetical order if the words were written backwards, follow the same process starting with the last letter of each word instead of the first.)

Start here ▼

anxiety   auction   ancient   axiomatic   auxiliary

All first letters are 'a' so they are in effect eliminated.

anxiety   auction   ancient   axiomatic   auxiliary

Now consider the 2nd letters, working through the alphabet:

anxiety   auction   ancient   axiomatic   auxiliary

a b c d e f g h i j k l m n
                             Two have 'n' as second letter
                             'anxiety' and 'ancient'

So now consider their 3rd letters: 'x' and 'c'
                                    'c' precedes 'x' in the alphabet,
                                    so write them down in that order
Alphabetical order: ancient, anxiety

Now consider the 2nd letter of the remaining three words, working through the alphabet:

auction   axiomatic   auxiliary

a b c d e f g h i j k l m n o p q r s t u
                             Two have 'u' as second letter
                             'auction' and 'auxiliary'
So consider their 3rd letters.
Alphabetical order: ancient   anxiety   auction   auxiliary
Leaving the remaining word as the last in the order.
Alphabetical order: ancient   anxiety   auction   auxiliary   axiomatic

It is now easy to identify the fourth in the list and to underline it as the correct answer.

ancient   anxiety   auction   **auxiliary**   axiomatic

(Other similar question types include arranging words in order by size, meaning or word length. In each case read through the list carefully and sort them into order from left to right. It is then possible to answer questions about individual positions.)

Now try these

If these words are placed in alphabetical order, which comes fourth?

1 cushion	customer	culinary	culture	cupboard	curable
2 apply	apple	ampere	applicant	ample	alpine
3 studious	strident	study	strictly	steady	street
4 thread	thorough	thoughtful	thrown	thrash	theatre

44 Putting letters in alphabetical order

Example

If the letters in the following word are arranged in alphabetical order which letter comes in the middle?

extravagant

How to do it

To place letters in alphabetical order slowly say the alphabet through in your head.
For each letter scan the word, and when the letter is present cross it through with a line and write it down.
Write the letters down in order, working from left to right.

Start here
▼
extravagant

a ?							extravagant aaa
b ?	c ?	d ?	e ?				extravagant aaae
f ?	g ?						extravagant aaaeg
h ?	i ?	j ?	k ?	l ?	m ?	n ?	extravagant aaaegn
o ?	p ?	q ?	r ?				extravagant aaaegnr
s ?	t ?						extravagant aaaegnrtt
u ?	v ?						extravagant aaaegnrttv
w ?	x ?						extravagant aaaegnrttvx
y ?	z ?						

From this order the middle position can be identified:

a a a e g <u>n</u> r t t v x

Now try these

If the letters in the following words are arranged in alphabetical order, which letter comes 7th?

1 dictionary   **2** frivolous   **3** comprehensive   **4** telescopic

45 Using letter and number codes to decode and encode words

Example

These number codes match the words given, but you are not told which code matches which word. Find and underline the code for PAIL.

7133	3162	5462	5143
PAIL	TALL	LANE	PINE

How to do it

Look carefully at the four words given.
You need to find one or two distinguishing features.
From these features you can begin to eliminate the different options.
There are usually several different ways of solving these question types.

Start here
▼

P A I L   T A L L   L A N E   P I N E

Observations: two words start with the same letter   **P**AIL and **P**INE

two words end with the same letter pair LA**NE** and PI**NE**

two words end with the same letter   PAI**L** and TAL**L**

only one word has a repeated letter   TA**LL**

Now look at the codes given:

7133   3162   5462   5143

Does any one of them have a repeated number?   *Yes*   71**33**

Therefore the code 7133 represents the word 'TALL'.

T   A   L   L

7   1   3   3

You are asked to find the code for 'PAIL'.

'PAIL' is the other word ending in 'L', so its code must end in 3.

So by elimination the code for 'PAIL' is <u>5143</u>.

Now try these

These number codes match the words given, but you are not told which code matches which word.

1 Find and underline the code for POUND.

329	359746	357	76594	65347	35297
PONDER	POUND	PUN	POD	DRONE	ROPED

2 Find and underline the code for TAPE.

4213	3142	4224	3213
PEEP	TEAT	TAPE	PEAT

3 Find and underline the code for FIRM.

2431	1324	6521	6352	6324
FIRM	FARE	REAM	MARE	FAIR

4 Find and underline the code for SCENE.

7698	73498	7669	75696
STAND	SEND	SCENE	SEEN

46 Using a symbol code to decode and encode words

Example

If ♣ ♦ ♠ ♥ is the code for R E A D, what is the code for A R E? _____

How to do it

Match the given word and its code very carefully together.
Then look at the new word to be encoded, or code word to be decoded.
Work through each letter in turn of the new word, working from left to right.
Right down each code symbol or letter as you work through. Remember to work from left to right to keep the letters or symbols in the correct order.

Start here
▼
♣ ♦ ♠ ♥
R E A D

Now encode the word A R E: A becomes ♠
                                  R becomes ♣
                                  E becomes ♦

The code for the word A R E is   ♠ ♣ ♦

Now try these

1 If ✳ ☆ ✚ → ○ ❣ ☆ is the code for BECAUSE,

what does the code ✚ ○ ✳ ☆ stand for? _____

what is the code for BEES? _____

2 If ☆ → ✳ ○ is the code for TEAR,

what does the code ✳ ○ ☆ stand for? _____

what is the code for RATE? _____

3 If ○ ❣ ☆ ✳ → is the code for STEAL,

what does the code → ✳ ❣ ☆ stand for? _____

what is the code for SALE? _____

47 | Answering questions from given information

The Browns live two houses away from the Wests.
The Wests are at the end of the road at house number 38.
The Wests are on the side of the road with even numbers.

What is the house number of the Browns?

How to do it

Read through the information very carefully, saying it aloud in your head.
You may then immediately work out what to do. If not, re-read the information making a note of each fact. A little diagram can often be helpful.
Sometimes one piece of information indicates that more than one option is possible. If so, note down both options; the following pieces of information will usually eliminate one of them which can then be crossed out, leaving the correct option.

Start here
▼
'The Browns live two houses away from the Wests.'

____   ____   the Wests   ____   ____

The Browns could live here or here

'The Wests are at the end of the road at house number 38.'

                    ____   ____   the Wests END OF ROAD

House number: ?   ?   38

'The Wests are on the side of the road with even numbers.'

                    ____   ____   the Wests END OF ROAD

House numbers – all even: 34   36   38

So the house next to the Wests must be 36, and **the Browns' house number is 34**.

Now try these

1 Andrew, Sam and Charles wore blue jeans.
   Sam, Charles and David wore navy jumpers.
   David, Stephen and Nick wore red shorts.
   Stephen, Andrew and Nick wore grey jumpers.

   Who wore red shorts and a navy jumper?

2 James, Sue and Tom have a bicycle.
   Sue, Tom and John like football.
   Ann, Jane and John do not have a bicycle.
   James, Jane and Ann do not like football.

   Who has a bicycle and does not like football?

3 Emily, Sarah and Susan have long hair.
   Susan, Anna and Kate have blue jackets.
   Emily, Jane and Sarah have red scarves.
   Kate, Jane and Anna have short hair.

   Who has long hair and a blue jacket?

4 The house is south of the big tree.
   The hill is east of the house.
   The house is east of the road.
   The pond is south of the house.

   Where is the big tree in relation to the pond?

48 | Making deductions from given information

Example

'Lions are animals. Animals are not stone.'

From these statements, underline the one statement that must be true.

Lions are cruel.
Lions are flesh.
Lions are not stone.
Lions are animals because they hunt.

How to do it

Read through the information given, saying it aloud in your head.
Then consider each of the statements in turn.
Compare each statement with the information given (**not** your own opinion or general knowledge).
Remember that you are looking for the statement which must be true.
Some of the statements may be true, but that alone does not qualify them as the answer.

Start here
▼
'Lions are animals. Animals are not stone.'

'Lions are cruel.'
Do the statements above say anything about lions?   **Yes**
                              and about cruelty?   **No**

Look at the next option.

'Lions are flesh.'
Do the statements above say anything about lions?   **Yes**
                               and about flesh?   **No**

Look at the next option.

'Lions are not stone.'
Do the statements above say anything about lions?   **Yes**
                             and about not stone?   **Yes**

Check this option.

Lions are animals and, as animals are not stone, <u>**lions are not stone**</u>.
This option must be true and is the correct answer.

Now try these

1 'Motorbikes are a form of transport. All forms of transport can move.'
   From these statements, underline the one statement that must be true.

   Motorbikes have two wheels.
   Motorbikes are fast.
   Motorbikes can move.
   Motorbikes are faster than cars.

2 'Eagles are birds. All birds have feathers.'
   From these statements, underline the one statement that must be true.

   Eagles have wings.
   Eagles are golden.
   Eagles have feathers.
   Eagles lay eggs.

3 'Yoghurt is made from milk. Milk contains calcium.'
   From these statements, underline the one statement that must be true.

   Yoghurt is good for you.
   Yoghurt is good for your bones.
   Yoghurt contains calcium.
   Yoghurt is flavoured with fruits.

4 'Wedgwood is fine china. Fine china is expensive.'
   From these statements, underline the one statement that must be true.

   Wedgwood is very famous.
   Fine china breaks easily.
   Wedgwood is made in Britain.
   Wedgwood is expensive.

Substituting numbers for letters

Example

If A = 1, B = 2, C = 3, D = 4 and E = 5 answer the following questions.

a) Find the value of the following word by adding the letters together.
BEAD ___

b) Give the answer to this sum as a letter.
B + D – E = ___

How to do it

a) Replace each letter in the given word with its corresponding number value.
Add together all of the numbers to find the answer.

b) Replace each letter with its corresponding number value. Then do the calculation and convert the numerical answer back into a letter. Look carefully at the signs in the calculation.

Start here
▼

a) B   E   A   D
2   5   1   4

2 + 5 + 1 + 4 = 12

The value of 'B E A D' is <u>12</u>.

b) B + D – E = ?

2 + 4 – 5 = 1

1 represents the letter A, so the answer is <u>A</u>.

Now try these

If A = 5, B = 7, C = 8, D = 9, E = 10 and F =11 answer the following questions.

a) Find the value of the following words by adding the letters together.

1 FEED ___   2 BADE ___   3 FACE ___   4 DEAF ___

b) Give the answer to these sums as letters.

5 B + C – E = ___   6 F + B – C = ___

7 F – D + A = ___   8 E – C + D = ___

50 General number work

Example

If eight is two more than half of this number, what is this number? _____

How to do it

Read through the information given very carefully, making a note of each stage.
To find what came before usually requires reversing the process stated.
If something is now more than the original, you need to subtract to find the original.
Conversely, if something is less than the original you will need to add on the difference to find the original.
If something has been doubled or trebled, that is multiplied by 2 or 3, then reverse the process and divide to find the original number.
Likewise, with a number which is now half, or a third, or a quarter of the original amount you reverse the process and multiply by 2, 3 or 4, respectively, to find the original quantity.

Start here
▼

If eight is two more ...   *ie the original number here is 2 less; 2 less than 8 is 6*
... than half of this number   *ie the original number is double the figure, that is 6 × 2 = 12*

Check your answer with the given information.

If the number is 12
            ... half of this number is 6
                        ... and two more than this number is 8

Yes, it does fit with the information given, so the answer is <u>12</u>.

Now try these

1 If twenty-four is six less than three times this number, what is the number? _____

2 If seventeen is four less than three times this number, what is the number? _____

3 If thirty-two is four more than four times this number, what is the number? _____

4 If thirteen is three less than twice this number, what is the number? _____

Answers

1
1 *Group A*: green, white; *Group B*: lemonade, milk; *Group C*: basketball, cricket
2 *Group A*: clarinet, oboe; *Group B*: drum, chime bar; *Group C*: double bass, viola
3 *Group A*: German, Dutch; *Group B*: ocean, lake; *Group C*: Belgium, Sweden
4 *Group A*: shorts, jumper; *Group B*: shampoo, bath-oil; *Group C*: cotton, velvet

2

1
Stationery	Flowers	Vegetables
envelopes	roses	potato
stamp	daffodil	turnip
	snowdrop	beetroot

2
Rivers	Countries	Cities
Thames	Chile	London
Severn	France	Paris

3
Currency	Measures of mass	Measures of time
dollars	kilogrammes	minutes
francs	gram	hours
euros	tonnes	seconds

4
Buildings	Materials	Furniture
bungalow	wood	wardrobe
mansion	plastic	table
cottage	steel	chair

3 1 dish, bowl 2 melody, tune 3 jog, trot 4 meadow, pasture

4 1 commence 2 thump 3 pounce 4 coast

5 1 friend, chum 2 red, scarlet 3 shed, hut 4 canopy, awning

6 1 tractor, chimney 2 picnic, knife 3 compass, palace 4 horse, bicycle

7 1 pineapple, banana 2 horse, pony 3 sparkle, twinkle 4 brave, courageous

8 1 mouse 2 yoghurt 3 hail 4 minim

9 1 hike 2 lamp 3 sleep 4 sorrow

10 1 untrustworthy 2 ill 3 concentrated 4 cruel

11 1 cheap, expensive 2 considerate, thoughtless 3 dangerous, safe 4 descend, ascend

12 1 short, tall 2 find, lose 3 old, young 4 reduce, increase

13 1 earth 2 lines 3 diamond 4 duck

14	**1** EAT	**2** HOT	**3** BIT	**4** ASH			

15	**1** h	**2** d	**3** l	**4** k	**5** ch	**6** sp	**7** en	**8** ge

16	**1** t	**2** d	**3** p	**4** w	**5** ch	**6** th	**7** en	**8** er

17	**1** PINEAPPLE	**2** CANAL	**3** CHEDDAR	**4** CYGNET

18	**1** seven, week	**2** snakes, lizards	**3** letters, alphabet	**4** Everest, Himalaya

19	**1** notice	**2** stretch	**3** verse	**4** metric

20	**1** main	**2** arrest	**3** streak	**4** opera

21	**1** feed	**2** bead	**3** dead	**4** beef

22	**1** seat, eats	**2** each, ache	**3** field, filed	**4** porter, report

23	**1** sunshine	**2** greenhouse	**3** handsome	**4** slipway

24	**1** water	**2** post	**3** butter	**4** sun

25	**1** care	**2** hole	**3** meat	**4** hero

26	**1** LANE	**2** HOLD	**3** FINE	**4** SHOW or SLOE
	5 MILE, MILK	**6** TEST, PEST or PENT, PANT or PENT, PEST	**7** THEN, THAN	**8** BELT, FELT or BELT, BELL

27	**1** sand	**2** slower	**3** pane	**4** rook

28	**1** can, send	**2** place, said	**3** tray, slowly	**4** cease, string

29	**1** f	**2** s	**3** p	**4** w

30	**1** CRANE	**2** PHEASANT	**3** FLOWER	**4** PAINTING

31	**1** slat	**2** money	**3** slice	**4** fatter

32	**1** ICED	**2** FEED	**3** FORT	**4** DEED

33	**1** children, books, library	**2** lady, path, castle	**3** wind, leaves, trees	**4** sun, seeds, ground

34 1 fields, sun   2 sun, ice-cream   3 for, to   4 robin, day

35 1 S U   2 U X   3 X Y   4 Q P

36 1 green   2 narrow   3 mice   4 south

37 1 cygnet   2 music   3 sow   4 ear

38 1 never, shut   2 poet, author   3 road, bridle-path   4 butterfly, frog

39 1 drink, thirst   2 grape, vineyard   3 building, architect   4 pond, lake

40

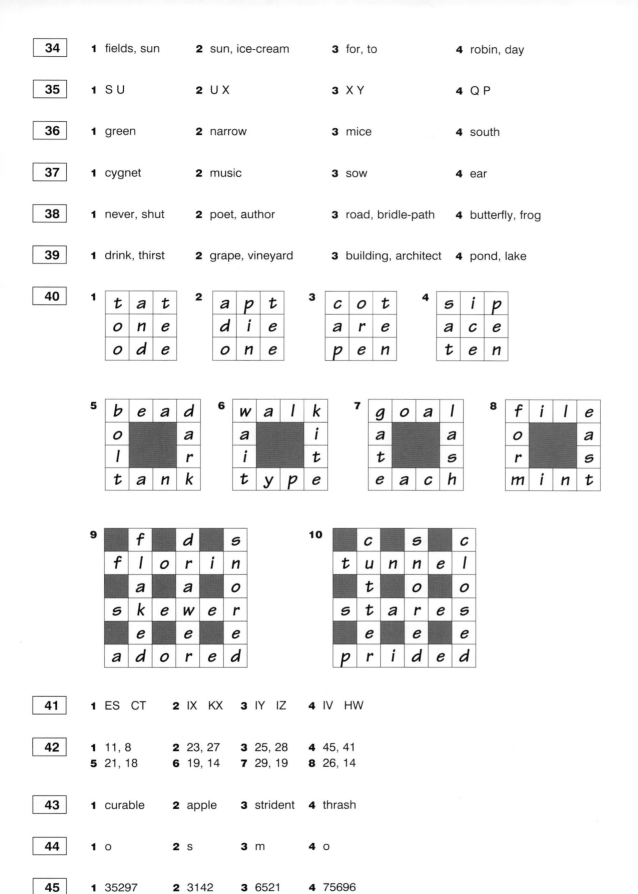

1
t	a	t
o	n	e
o	d	e

2
a	p	t
d	i	e
o	n	e

3
c	o	t
a	r	e
p	e	n

4
s	i	p
a	c	e
t	e	n

5
b	e	a	d
o			a
l			r
t	a	n	k

6
w	a	l	k
a			i
i			t
t	y	p	e

7
g	o	a	l
a			a
t			s
e	a	c	h

8
f	i	l	e
o			a
r			s
m	i	n	t

9
	f		d		s
f	l	o	r	i	n
	a		a		o
s	k	e	w	e	r
	e		e		e
a	d	o	r	e	d

10
	c		s		c
t	u	n	n	e	l
	t		o		o
s	t	a	r	e	s
	e		e		e
p	r	i	d	e	d

41 1 ES CT   2 IX KX   3 IY IZ   4 IV HW

42 1 11, 8   2 23, 27   3 25, 28   4 45, 41
5 21, 18   6 19, 14   7 29, 19   8 26, 14

43 1 curable   2 apple   3 strident   4 thrash

44 1 o   2 s   3 m   4 o

45 1 35297   2 3142   3 6521   4 75696

46   **1** cube, ✳ ☆ ☆ ❢   **2** art, ○ ✳ ☆ →   **3** late, ○ ✳ → ☆

47   **1** David   **2** James   **3** Susan   **4** north

48   **1** Motorbikes can move.   **2** Eagles have feathers.
         3 Yoghurt contains calcium.   **4** Wedgwood is expensive.

49   a) **1** 40   **2** 31   **3** 34   **4** 35
      b) **5** A   **6** E   **7** B   **8** F

50   **1** 10   **2** 7   **3** 7   **4** 8